DARE SAY

DARE SAY

POEMS BY
TOD MARSHALL

The University of Georgia Press
Athens

Reissued edition published in 2016
by the University of Georgia Press
Athens, Georgia 30602
www.ugapress.org
© 2002 by Tod Marshall
All rights reserved
Designed by April Leidig-Higgins
Set in Monotype Garamond and Gill Sans by
    Bookcomp, Inc.

Most University of Georgia Press titles are
available from popular e-book vendors.

Printed digitally

The Library of Congress has cataloged the previous
edition of this book as follows:
Marshall, Tod.
Dare say : poems / by Tod Marshall.
59 p. ; 22 cm.
ISBN 0-8203-2462-0 (alk. paper)
I. Title.
PS3613.A777 D37 2002
811'.6—dc21   2002008740

2016 paperback reissue ISBN 978-0-8203-5053-0

CONTENTS

1   **ONE**

3   Eclipse

15   **TWO**

17   Manifest and Destiny

18   Storm

19   Lightning,

20   And This, Following the Weather

21   Botticelli

26   Untitled

28   St. Joan among the Pines

29   Of

31   Nocturne

32   Choir

33   **THREE**

35   Prodigal

37   Apollinaire on the Great Plains

38   Yes, There Are Times

39   Breakfast

40   Morning, with Monkeys

41   St. Jude and the Tomatoes

42   After Kandinsky

51   Metaphysic, with Blue

52   Metaphysic, with Bird

53   Metaphysic, with Applebee's

57   Notes

59   Acknowledgments

ONE

"Always the seer is the sayer."

EMERSON

Eclipse

The Variations

Aria

Refuse cruelty.

Hear the branches' illiterate quivering.

Behold the moon's eloquent shine.
An angel
whispers in her ear,
acute angles of folded wings.

Memorize the steady chant of bells.
Watch her swell.

I

Like Hildegard of Bingen:

"A little later, I had a marvelous and mystical vision; all my inner organs
were swollen and upset and the sensations of my body were no longer
felt. For my consciousness had been transformed, as if I no longer knew
myself, as if raindrops were falling from the hand of God upon my soul."

II

An eloquent music envelops her,
makes her belly swell and shine. Perhaps
it is

III

Bach, the rocking of branches in a gentle wind, air rhythmically flexing in gusts as if the universe were just a pair of healthy lungs. As if the branches, around dusk, tire of the various exercises of contrition and release sacrificial leaves, begging insects for a few moments of peace. As if autumn were just another story festering in the mind of God. Like heaven, electricity, and the invention of music that does not end. The ground is sprinkled with such abandoned wealth. A night sky littered with stars that once flashed like knives, switch blades aimed at carving out the moon's intrusion into rational order, the swollen tongue of a gentle wind—that same one again—those sharp guardians of history's fugue, the return of a hopeful melody that refuses the "lewd cycle," as Spengler called it, of conception, blossom, the final fireworks of fruition, and the lengthy death-shiver sardonically called, tongue tucked against the cheek, civilization.

IV

The first sermon is not a story.
Saints embrace a sort of mortification,
a partial articulation of the soul's
inherent anarchy: to bend back
desire's steady insistence, to sit
atop a deep well, wants and needs
literally swelling toward the rim,
scaly claws skittering against
the intricate stonework; perched
there, wielding smooth wooden staves,
shoving at illiterate lust, refusing
compulsions into a long fall
after which they regroup,
learn to worship the moon,
and begin to crawl again.

V

History: The swelling movement at the end of a musical phrase was characteristic of the period after the Baroque.

Commentary: Wagner's lip curling with disgust as he dubs such sounds the clatter of princely dishes.

VI

Dualism is a cruelty,
the literal refusal
of God and world.
Eloquence as union,
whispers folding
through the angles
of the ear: memorize
the shining angel
in her swelling body
that *is* her swelling
body. The steady,
quivering bells
chant the same.

VII

His fingers momentarily linger over the keys of a harpsichord, black and white pattern seething with symmetry, great German knuckles swollen into Trinitarian regions of fantastic genius. A few weeks before, he had composed the *Goldberg Variations* meant to soothe a patron steadily to sleep. Linger, and then begin to play. Beautifully, and yet halfway through those fingers refuse familiarity, realize that repetition is the cruel core of loss, that there is little wonder in this slow, cyclical eclipse of the world, and so he eloquently improvises, plays for hours until his young second wife, swollen with child, calls him downstairs, casually asks, "What was it you were working on, what brought such sweat to your brow?"

VIII

Hildegard wrote:

"When in accordance with the secret order and will of God, at an appropriate time rightly determined by divine providence, the child in its mother's swollen womb has received the spirit, it shows by the movement of its body that it is alive."

IX

Cruelty shaped to a story
invites the act to happen
again. Swollen words
whispered into the acute
folds of an eloquent sentence.
Hear the moon's steady hum.
Find refusal in the illiterate,
the body's quivering, the
angelic chanting of bells.

X

The next sermon is not a song.
Electricity clicking through wires
becomes visible, for a second, when that
God's-wrath-crashed bolt of swollen light
strikes the local transformer,
and power lines change into a tempestuous net
of sparks that showers nearby houses
and announces the child's arrival.

XI

History: Music remains alive to intuition, and Bach's eloquent art finds international response among those who are sensible to metaphysical realities, whatever their intellectual predispositions may be.

Commentary: The sky a gauzy blue stained with grey smoke: a *cantata* performed by ragged skeletons in a courtyard. Enthusiastic applause, the metaphysics of barbed wire.

XII

Cruelty refuses eloquence
to fold beyond acute angles.
Wings chanting air
swell the memory of wind,
a steady whispering
that branches throughout
an illiterate angel's body.

XIII

She rubs her stomach and says
the child will be here soon.

XIV

Sing: The belly is an altar,
        the belly is a fruit.
        The baby likes to kick
        with his tiny foot.

xv

Chant: to stroke the globe of skin, to press palms
against the arched abdomen, to see the swollen navel
steadily become a tiny stem atop the heavenly bloat
that collapses, compacts, and squeezes through
the acute angles of that illiterate cave of dreams,
and wakens in a world so bright the lungs flutter
then loose a scream.

xvi

And Hildegard wrote:

"I saw a very bright fire which was incomprehensible, swollen, wholly living, and appearing as if it were totally alive. The flame of the fire was an airy color, and it was blazing violently in a gentle wind. And I saw this flame lighten in color and give forth a bolt of lightning, the bright fire, blazing violently in a gentle wind."

xvii

The uncollected sermon.
Behold the stained glass:
a Virgin's blue robe,
her swollen stomach hidden
within eloquent folds of cloth.
Light's steady shine
through angelic white wings.
Memorize the green, blue,
and red panes. Whisper
and they shatter.

XVIII

Kapelmeister, twenty children, two wives, and official appointments all
  over the land:
What notes eloquently capture the loss of a child?
Only eleven of yours ever ran, caressed the keyboard, or plucked at the
  strings of an earthly instrument.
Johann Christoph and Maria Sophia, twins dead right after birth.
Leopold Augustus, dead before the end of a year.
Christian Gottlieb, dead at three.
Johann August Abraham, dead within a day.
Christiane Dorothea, dead at the age of one.
Christiane Benedicta, dead after three days.
Ernestus Andreas, dead on All Saints Day, his first.
A thematic recursion? They said you composed a six-part fugue in your
  head.
Or, after the first, does it feel like an Old Testament curse, like wrestling
  angels, a plague of sores upon swollen skin, like tucking the sacrificial
  dagger in the folds of your robe and turning to the steep path, knowing
  no voice will refuse the blade's awful arc, that the only whisper will be
  your arm's cut across the sky?

XIX

History: The count commissioned him to write soothing music to relieve
the tedium of sleepless nights.

Commentary: *music is pure narration, a story that can't be told.*

XX

On the Trinity, Hildegard wrote:

"The Lord is brightness and this brightness swells and flashes forth and
in this flashing forth is fire and these three are one."

XXI

The final sermon.
"Lyvwire,"
the license plate
reads. Live
as in electricity, god-
son of generator
and necessity, held
up on those lines,
liquefied stars
rushing through swollen
cables. Or live
like the concert
in the park, *2nd*
Brandenburg
and *The Goldberg Variations:*
Bach's eloquent returns.
The audience applauding
and grabbing jackets
and purses, folding up blankets
as they hurry to cars,
trying to avoid
swollen traffic,
even though the black-
tied musicians
haven't finished their bows.

XXII

Unlike Hildegard, who wrote music,
lived cloistered, and meditated for days
on the exact shade of angelic light,
she swells and gives birth.

XXIII

Behold the angelic whispering
of wings, sparrows refusing
the cat's eloquent threat.
They land in the branches,
clean feathers, and gather
debris into a nest, steadily
swelling clump of lint
and string, angular shine
of a bent paper clip, a tatter
of egg carton that looks
like a bell, an illiterate moon.

XXIV

After the healing, she takes up painting,
portraiture of the cruel ones. Their victims:
children catching a last glimpse of sky,
gauzy blue stained with grey smoke.
A man holds open the metal door.
Slight brush stroke, a bit more work
on the mustache, a crinkled nervous tic
at the corner of his mouth. Blending
oils, she finds the right shade for steel
helmets, a color that somehow captures
the moment of crushed hope, the quivering
that is almost-extinguished life. A steady hand
that bares clarity, bristles in the details and
reminds the viewer to refuse repetition's force.

XXV

Spengler said humanity is a "beast of prey." To say otherwise is to be "a beast of prey without teeth." The leaves drop and will drop again, gentle wind rippling through branches swollen by colorful fall. Lungs, liver, splendorous guts, double helix telling the tale of civilization, the tale of life without wings, a cruel narrative with no use for *is*.

XXVI

History: The Germans' steady approach refused any quarter for the civilians who tried to flee the area. It was, one Belgian said, as if the wings, the boots, the gunfire, and shells had synthesized into a cruel symphony of destruction.

Commentary: And then there was silence, as if and silence, was and silence, just silence.

XXVII

Steadily refuse the cruel bells.
Fold quivering hands.
Clench them to fists. Then
unbend the fingers
into open palms. Memorize
the angles of the angel's wings,
a woodcut on the altar,
how he whispers into the virgin's
ear. Illiterate boots will chant.
They can do nothing to stop
the eloquent swelling of bodies,
the moon beholden,
offering its shine.

XXVIII

And wings summon the angels
who offer this simple sermon,
present tense throughout,
that narrates, sings, and stutters:
There are nights that drive the stars
from the sky, send the moon
behind clouds of smoke, nights
when cruelty refuses
every eloquent and illiterate cry
of pain and keeps pressing the blade.
They speak and stop, and the light
they leave pardons no darkness,
embraces all that shines.

XXIX

A sequence that comes to an end.
Impregnation, gestation, and birth.
No ceaseless speech whispers behind our backs,
nothing cares to keep our stories alive.
Listen. You'll hear the electric clatter
of collapsing stars. To refuse that sound
as anything other than soothing—a mother's song
over the crib of a sleeping child—is to accept
the acute eloquence of the moon, the folding
away of cruelty, the love of illiterate wings.

xxx

A finished self-portrait—memorize
her eyes, the moment of conception,
rain falling from the hand of God. In her posture,
the fierce determination of birth.

She hangs it near a window, allows paint
to dry. The child sleeps, just barely
shaded from the sun; recorded violins
drift up from downstairs.

Probably Brahms, appropriate
for autumn, the fade to dusk, a century
where any story might be true. At night,
when the child cries, she nurses him on the couch,

listening to the steady music of mouth
and swollen nipple, illiterate
and insistent—supple lips, strong jaw—
shaping an eloquence that eclipses the self.

Aria Refrain

Refused cruelty quivers.

Illiterate wingfold of angels
whispers in your ear.

Behold the moon's memorable shine
through acute angles
of stars and sky.

Hear steady bells,

an eloquent chant
that swells.

TWO

"The light
  Of the closed pages, tightly closed, packed against each other
  Exposes the new day,

  The narrow, frightening light
  Before a sunrise."

GEORGE OPPEN

Manifest and Destiny

If wind scolding branches
says more
than *no*
and *the body must break
from the soul,* brings

more than spattering rain
and lightning
sparking small fires,
then the wound
will consume
those last words
divvied

among friends,
fester,
and burst apart like a
century, a boom
town after the silver runs
out, the weight of ethical pledges
muttered on a sinking ship
    (the raft let loose to sea,
the men soon to eat
each other's skin and gristle,
gnaw white bones). Branches
batter windows, break and fall
through windows, no one
to clean up,
no one to admire shattered glass.

Storm

Happened thus: a woman rushing across the street
    drops a vase and blossoms scatter, confetti-
      like, wedding-like, explosion-like, too,
fragments of flower and glass, shattered church
    windows, sheared-off sheet rock, splintered wood,
      a terrorist attack, police action, or maybe
just a pick-up truck t-boning a Volkswagen bug.
    Regardless, the sirens are springtime, too,
      an erotic eruption of purple slopes, pink
curlicues, the arch of emerging petals, glass blooming
    on black pavement, clouds in each shard,
      the sharp pain of taking root, stamen
and pistil, sun's merciful fusion
    coupled to the bright blast
      of those awful bombs: the first drops
wash petals away—purples, pinks, and reds—
    but green stains the imagination,
      and broken glass echoes the sky,
and the last breath of the driver
    impaled upon his steering wheel
      hushes wind for a moment,
slows the relentless
    storm before the loosened thunder, light-
      ning, a jagged flowering, tears of glass
like slivers of sun, slices of body,
    blossoms
      blown up and falling to earth.

Lightning,

the only intelligence rain gave,
that first burst a scintillating flash of self-knowledge.
We saw our bodies, pale starfish-feet
dragged from the sea, our sexes
like swollen fruit left too long on the vine,
bellies thick witnesses to slips in propriety,
chests two expansive maps of the wide, dry plains,
and our oh so lovely hands
catching rain in cups we must drink from
to deny the judgment of common sunshine,
the rationality that evaporates an impulse,
a sudden touch, the pounding rain.

And This,
Following the Weather

Rain on the roof
baptizes a mysterious absence

I thought at first was her voice, later realize
is just a loneliness of intense listening,

a moment I suppose will be remembered.
Drops linger on blades of grass,

clasp newfound sunlight, and let a prism loose.
I call this endless possibility.

Sometimes I mean it.
She left yesterday, water falling

from the sky, forty-eight hours
since the abortion, and old reliable dusk

announces the simple plot of night.
Skies clear for the sliced moon

and the stars, oh yes, the stars.

Botticelli

ı A Story

A woman went to Florence.
In a run-down chapel, a hand-painted sign: Botticelli's Grave.
She followed the arrows to a small cemetery where children asked for
   handouts and an old man demanded an entrance fee.
She paid.
Asked which one was his.
The man claimed the name had worn off,
that the *pioggia* is so constant, the water, the rain,
that no one knows for sure,
that no one should.

ıı Bits of History

Name: Alessandro di Mariano Filipepi.
Born: 1445.
Around the corner, the Vespuccis, named after brown wasps that looked
   like tiny flies.
Their eldest son, Amerigo, charted a continent.
They asked Alessandro for paintings.
He gave them one, never finished another.
He never slept with a woman.
One night he woke from a lusty dream of marriage and walked the alleys
   of Florence till dawn.
Savonarola had him lugging canvasses of beautiful nudes, heaping them
   on a pile to be purified in penitent flames.
Later, the painter would walk these same streets, old and alone, clutching
   his crutches.
The pile was high.
The crowd watched them burn, flames reflected in their eyes.

III *Primavera*

A lost paradise lingers just outside the frame.
You must have this faith. If you do,
wisdom shudders in the vibrant cries
of a lover pinned beneath your body. Leaves
become more than another coloring of death,
of loss, of our drastically fast lives. The graces
are complacently painted, only ceremonious.
Realize the slick edges of seraphim would otherwise
hurt us. It has nothing to do with refuting love
or the delicious form of the body, only
the religious imagination pushed to limits, defined
in curve, line, swollen abdomen, and the small globes
you could hold and call *breast.* Choose
to give richness to the fluid movement
of time, the delicate smell of decay,
a man's sweat, woman's scent, that musky twinning
you might call *fuck,* might call *love,* a celebration
of heat errantly labeled *desire.*
The myth of union, legend of hunger.
Zephyr lovely and frightening.

iv Therefore,

I said, slurring,
Botticelli had a mainline to God.
She laughed, said he'd ended up
another puppet of a church gone wrong.
Cut out the false angst and look at
Braque and Picasso, even Kandinsky.
The real masters. I finished my wine,
sharply considered her hand
on the thin-stemmed glass, the dark red liquid,
the lines of her fingers classically correct,
and slowly said she was incredibly wrong,
that the moderns knew only colors.

v *The Birth of Venus*

Probably one of the most famous paintings in Western Art, it combines
elements of pagan voluptuousness with a strictly Botticellian anatomy.
Yet, despite the obvious classical inspiration, this Venus is wistful in ap-
pearance, chaste and patiently awaiting the cloak one of the Hours is about
to cast around her bare body. Finished approximately 1485, this piece
shows the exaggerated proportions that made him famous: a honeyed
torrent of cascading hair, the exquisite female form, the decorous place-
ment of her hands. All serve to transport the viewer far beyond the realm
of anatomical accuracy.

vi Details

The next morning she told me the whole story.
Autumn. A strong breeze. Wind rippling branches,
strain of leaf-stem, the sudden release and flutter.
Sun through the window brighter than I'd have liked.
Her mouth struggled with the first few words.
I imagined birds singing, noticed the fine blue bowl
on her redwood dresser, the black cabinet
hung full of dresses, skirts, and jackets, littered
with colorful shoes. She only stopped
to ask for a glass of water. I returned from the sink;
she emptied the glass in three quick swallows.
I stared at the shoes and listened.

vii confession is the most dangerous act of faith

Ficino: Faith is love without reason.
Savonarola: Only the love of God.
Everything else is hellish blasphemy.
Pico Mirandola: Beauty hides in every block
of marble, every empty canvas timidly waiting
for the first brush stroke, the initial chiseling
to bring the form to life, placed by God
for the artist to reveal. And yet, each nude beauty
instills a longing unfulfilled by the lofty walls of religion.
The eating of bread, sipping of wine too distant
from the bestial desires that lured men
and women to fuck among the trees. And worse.
The peasant girl dragged by the Florentine merchant
to a grove just beyond the fields, her dirty cheeks
flushed from rape. He swaggered away
to ride his horse and arrive in time for Mass.
She was left to bleed in the fertile dirt.
This is what she said: the beggar man closed
    the metal gate and told me to take off my clothes.

Knife glitter, cold mud: it was quick. The *polizia*
did nothing. One detective said I was *stupido*
for being there alone, lucky I wasn't cut.
She also remembered the pamphlet from the museum
that said Savonarola was hung and burnt, the body
quickly catching fire while plump Florentine women
perched on balconies fiddled with their hair.
She finished and asked for more water.
I filled her glass. Outside, the wind ripped
loose a few more leaves that rose, for a moment,
and fell beyond the window's frame.

VIII

She shrugs when I mention his work,
says "did you know his name means 'little barrel,'
that his fingers were unnaturally long and thin?"
Then she shifts the conversation to a consideration
of the haunting brush-dabs of Van Gogh, Klimt's
obsession with pubic hair, even Turner's fiery seascapes.
Ruskin's angel. "The sun is God" she quotes and laughs,
reaching for the pot to pour more coffee. I'm silent,
once again listening, unable to say anything worth her faith,
to change the conversation to something contemporary,
or silly, to something that will not last, struck dumb
by the tireless shove of desire, brutal beauty,
and the pure displacement of grace.

Untitled

And the painter writing again about God,
the model having left for the day
with a sore back to consider
his request to paint her pissing,
water and earth moving through body,

the body moving earth and water
through slimy chambers, and in his letter
God has become that which christens
the landscape to life—a shepherd penning
his flock, a wagon creaking beneath

its load of peasants, a boy
trying to net a frog in a muddy ditch,
dusk coming on, somewhere
a bell calling others to dinner,
the fields disappearing to darkness,

each leaf, then branches and whole
trees becoming darker shades
in the dark night, until only the painter
remains after having sat by wagon ruts
all day, looking, looking for God

but only seeing God-in-things—
and so when she agrees, he paints
her buttocks with blunt smudges
that almost capture the splash
of piss in the pot, his half-smile

and riveted attention like the boy's
as he stalks through dusky water,
a net descending, pinning the frog
to the ditch-bank, and the bell stops,
and stars emerge, a spray

of silvery-white, and later,
when the model's gone, he paints
over her portrait, two mules
pulling a wagon, peasants swaying along
in its wooden palm, a boy on his back

daydreaming by a small ditch, gazing
into the sinking sun, feet flecked
with mud, trees slouched as if listening
to his slow breathing, wagon ruts
like wrinkles on a man's face.

St. Joan among the Pines

Summer storms and the forest burns,
old cedars exploding like hundreds
of small suns, mile after mile of scorched
pine like charred spears jutting up, the blackened
landscape a purgatory for desire, metaphoring
apocalypse, a lie: new shoots poke through
in September. Elk graze the burn
soon to be buried by feet-deep snow.
And Joan? She sings spark and flame, sings
smoke into notes that rise to air. Sings green.
Lightning comes, fires loose themselves
through the heart of the forest. Extinguish nothing.
The elk graze, mule deer lumber among stumps.
And the music: You must torch your life.

Of

A boat's wake against the shore,
steady speech of green and blue,
a felt language that tumbles small stones,
even loosens a few larger rocks
to answer the water's voice.

The woodpecker knows *trunk* is noun for maker,
Believes *rat-tat-tat* against that
which gives up ants
and mites and grubs is a simple hymn.
Of drama: a man may think all this,

may say *listen* to a woman he loves, his finger
pointing at a willow sagging over the water,
and she might glance at the same branches,
the place on the trunk where the beak
scars soft wood, might even see the red-headed bird

and reply, "Yes, I understand," and think
"the water yields to the shore's pull,"
or "the mites and grubs and ants
know the persistent woodpecker's success,
for a moment, and then the long silence

of stone." She may grab at a strand of hair
to tuck behind her ear and wonder
how she ever loved this man
with his finger groping the sky. *Rat-tat-tat*
goes the bird, water calms

to a pebbly murmur,
and the couple's loneliness is only spoken
in the mossy language of tumbling stones. The lake
goes smooth at the last boat's docking,
receives the moon, the stars, the crickety hum of night,

and the man and woman walk back
to where they lie down, stare at swirls
in the plaster ceiling, and sleep. Of prayer:
fierce bird, gouge that wood
and let water whisper words

that are luminous enough
to move the lovers to waking.

Nocturne

Three angels, two gathered beneath a greater third.
The place—a parochial school courtyard,
a cathedral's well-trimmed garden, or even

a bronze monument to some spectacle of suffering.
But no, bronze won't allow this delicacy,
which must be white. And the moon

invites you to slide your hand slowly
over wings, to forget yourself in chiseled feathers
and such smooth stone. *Only alabaster,*

you half mumble, half moan, seduced by light,
the godlike proposition of bodies.

Choir

But mud covers the angels,
a perfect disguise for feathery wings.
Try it. Smear yourself with sloppy handfuls,
scoop dark clumps from puddles,
paint your face and arms, drop
globs on feet and toes, and slip
into the streets, smile at everyone,
and they'll ignore you as only the holy
are ignored. A choice: learn to fly,
to lift your body by the strength of muscle and bone,
or live with drying mud and a song,
that familiar human singing,
the refrain that ends in dirt, dirt, dirt.

THREE

"Dazzling and tremendous how quick the sun-rise would kill me,
If I could not now and always send sun-rise out of me."

WHITMAN

Prodigal

And if out the window
peonies glow white beneath moon and stars,
and traffic's rhythmic hum
occasionally riffs into sirens
ricocheting against house fronts—
cicadas, an insistent snapping like the double helix
cracked against the sky; the moon, a pale bruise on the night's dark skin—
then the longing for light we call love
might shrink in that small silence-that-is-not-silence
and harden into a dark seed
I could carry in my pocket
across city limits and state lines, through metal detectors,
over countries and continents, oceans and peaks,
back, back, to that home before home,
quiet garden where peonies flare like stars.

Or if I walk out my front door,
down the sidewalk to the city center,
steel and concrete eclipsing the night sky,
and sit and wait for the morning rush
of those called to work, that laboring through
intent on arrival
at a cubicle or desk,
and ask each of the men and women
what ancient seed they lug around in their hearts,
will they embrace me
like a lost now-found son
or turn away
as if I were another crazy come to claim their time?
If each window opens to a blossoming world,
and blossoms are cousins to muscles and bone,
to brain, cousins to skin that hugs our guts
and carries us toward that uncle-to-all, death,
then each window latch, each click of steel,

slide of glass, throwing open of doors to inhale the night air
reveals sharp stars
and the barely visible layer of god-dust,
blue and sweet and shimmering,
convincing eyes and ears and heart
that at the center, a muscle flexes and beats,
cosmic blossom that sparks, flowers to fire,
and burns.

Apollinaire on the Great Plains

Distance is unlivable
when wheat fields remind us
that we are small,

a thought that scalds our brains
like liquid stars.
But the wound only hurts

for a while. We
have wings and eyes. We
see and fly.

And when the sun cuts
the furrows' throat, we
seed, we sway, we rise.

Yes, There Are Times

when you hold your breath against a moment's passing—
the dropped glass suspended above cement,
loosed arrow yet to pierce the target, a thrown stone just a hole
in water prior to the widening ripple. Say it:
A woman sleeps, comforter and sheets
holding her shoulders in a cottony embrace.
Outside the window, sliced melon on a silver tray,
then lemon wedge plunked in the middle
of a pink salmon steak: sunrise.
Outside the window, sparrows rattle like castanets
and launch themselves to air. Outside the window,
the once again damp daily news
lands with a papery thud
in the dew-soaked grass. A woman sleeps,
and you sit at the foot of the bed, pleasantly obsessed
with the thought that a woman sleeps
without worry or care, sleeps toward that moment—
and here there will be those who hem and haw,
shuffle their feet, and look away. Pity their disbelief
because she sleeps toward that moment when the world
will stutter and pause, the lungs' imminent flexing
hitching against their release, raucous heart
holding its persistent beat, reckless sparrows
hovering midair, even the planets
bucking against their cosmic spin, as she rises from the comforter and
    sheets
and stretches. Yes, those muscles; yes, those tendons;
the beloved's body of water and light and bone. Yes,
the long loneliness of night is over,
for she stretches and lets the day begin.

Breakfast

Snow on the sidewalk,
elegant icicles
dangling from drain gutters.

This is not about the cold,
only burnt toast,
more coffee brewing,

and orange juice poured in a glass.
These and the tinny clink
and clank of silverware

rinsed in the sink
herald a gentle end
to morning. Remember the sound

of *juice,* bacon crackling
in the pan. Remember the smooth sheen
of fragile wings. Ours to touch.

Morning, with Monkeys

First cup of coffee, ribbon of rising steam,
and the music of monkeys,
Siamangs at a nearby zoo, that hurl themselves

through air, dexterous digits clutching cords
suspended between smooth poles, and stop
opposite each other atop those wooden perches,

and stare—long pause to fill inflatable throat sacs—
and a single note plunges from the heart
of *Symphalangus syndactylus,* black gibbon,

plain crazy jumping monkey, and the bass call erupts
from one, a high-pitched cacophonous frenzy
from the other, and they vault and swing

and ricochet through air. The trash truck beep-beeps
as it backs up. *Take it all,* the monkeys say, *take it all
away* with a hai, hai, hai, and a ho, ho. Cold cup

of coffee: a lion roars, another answers,
and the illiterate sun pours forth the day with a hee, hee,
and a hoo, hoo, and a yum, yum.

St. Jude and the Tomatoes

Although at the market, the produce aisle, surrounded
by a palette of fruit and vegetables, luscious pears,
juicy tangerines, the tiny blue muscles of plump huckleberries,
tomatoey reds, cucumbery greens, the faded sheen of waxed
apples, and so on, flavors recalled by the always hungry tongue,
a bald boy stares at you, and you need to shout or sing
at his lost hair: *St. Jude, we are all wandering*
stars with no one to snatch us from the fire. But tomatoes
call you back to your squeeze-and-choose, and when you look again,
he's gone. Abandon your life to a shout, announce that ache
for a song: say you shall sing *o peach* and sing,
say you shall shout *damn the silence of saints* and shout.
Feel *o my child* and feel. Say you shall act.

After Kandinsky

Proem: what must be written

is a poem of Kandinsky's spears
of particular things sharp and changing
of faith in the place of places

a poem in which the heart may rest
find solace in the kindness of balding men
and the lyrical hands of mothers

a colorful poem
with a subtle use of heavenly blue
a delicate shading of earthly yellow

a poem full of connections to everyday rituals
like coffee
stroking the arch of a cat's back

like syntax
a poem that fixes the body
to a specific place

of points and lines and planes
and yet moves to celestial music
a poem that tests

one 15th century truth
"Whoever loves much does much"
a poem that glistens with an unmatched insistence

a poem that arrives on time
and demands everyone
nail it to the wall.

i Hagiography

Perhaps it was 1413
when à Kempis wrote that.
He ended up trapped,
three feet of Dutch dirt
pinning a coffin's lid
and then a last-second
twitch of the worn-out form
he'd so often struggled
against. Two hundred years
later shovels uncovered
a simple wooden box.
Astonishment among some,
satisfaction for the scoffers:
his rotted body
gazing away from light.

ii Sketching

              clues to understand
                     our brutal century
                     its random calamities
                 among stroke
          and streak of pencil
              eraser friction rubbing away
what wasn't meant to be
                     and stroke again
              like this—
         glimpse of sun
           a gauzy morning light
ignites silver
          in the glistening threads
                 of a soon to be gone
                             spider web
          stretched between two houses
             as if aesthetics

took precedence
            always.

Kandinsky continually sketched
                    eschatological drawings—
        the revelation of St. John
                        gatherings of other Saints—
        between 1911 and 1914.
        The oil paintings based
                on the sketches
        are consumed by abstraction
        the spiritualization
            of the content
                    one critic claims.
Wind strains the spindly threads
            which give enough
                to resist
        snapping.
            They shine as matter
            and sunlight
        a filamental mesh
                to catch meat.

        An angel
    heralds warnings
        with a yellow horn
    and a white star
                drops like a stone—in *All Saints*
                Kandinsky's crucifix
                    is small
            hidden by the action
                    of the canvas: circling dove
                    radiant butterfly
                    and blossoming sunflower
        the angel's swollen cheeks
                    pink and round
    trumpet something substantial

something a watcher of webs
hungers to touch
vague
yet specifically located
at the axis
of those same threads
a hunger as urgent
as the expressions
of sinners dragged to hell
in Michelangelo's *Last Judgment*
for instance
where the blurred auto-
biographical face
drips
in the hand of an awful demon
and is still
a face.

III The Reason for Spears

has nothing to do
with sunlight
on raised steel
or artfully carved
spear heads

only gore
the torn flesh
fierce puncture
release of pressure
called skin

as metal enters
the exposed side

the reason for spears
is their honest intent

iv Kandinsky's Notes

"the non-objective painter
reacts intuitively
to a superior influence
free to follow a higher evolution
beyond the pretense of make believe"

But garbage
is a problem. Dig holes. Float it
on barges. Let the incinerators
burn night and day.

It still piles up.

Listen:
the resilient candor of wild roses
instills faith. Especially in a city.
Corn could grow here. One stalk
and then a few ears, tassels of silk,
one green sprout at a time.

And tomatoes.
O globes, o lovely tomatoes,
bright and red, erotic
circularity
luminous beneath the civil streetlights.

O dissolvable things.

v Two Refutations and a Proof

"In grey there is no possibility of movement."
Thick mist.
Shells shuffled by the tide.
A gull rising from sand
pivoting
toward ocean.

"Absolute green is the most restful color."
Fallen
hedge apples in wet grass—
pale jewels—
they glisten!

"Blue is the most heavenly color."
Crater Lake—
the cliffs form a deep cup
filled with brilliant blue—
an urge to jump
a thirst.

vi *Lyrical* (1911)

Chinese calligraphy formed this horse.
Gashed nostrils, wind-swept mane,
the tense arch of the horse's neck.

The rider is color.
A sunny helmet, bright yellow pantaloons,
the green fluid sail of shirt.

They are speed.
They are strokes.

And the horse readies its legs for the stretch
and the jockey needs no spurs
and the smooth and fast-paced track goes blue
and the horse pinches his eyes against the wind
and the horse's haunch explodes like a majestic spread of wings
and the horse's tail flutters like the plume of a bird
and the jockey knows green is the blur of grass
and the blue of the track is water and air
and the jockey knows

they are speed.
They are strokes.
The horse and rider
leave form and line
far behind.

VII

Mimesis is a shot at God.
       Abstraction
             a shot at the world.
   Neither can hold
      movement
         or the blooming flower
             although
        Da Vinci's drawings of musculature
      extension and rotation
or the study by Muybridge
            of the galloping horse
       every tendon
        each muscle
     flexing and stretching
      bunching
        like cords of braided sun
       just beneath the skin

come close
almost as close
as the explosions of color
Kandinsky stitched together
called *Black Lines*—
stem-like sketches
flecked
all over the canvas
we might think of
as broken forms.

We breathe
and breathing mimics
the muscular movement
of God
for awhile
and then
creatures of dust
and a spark
we do what God
can never do
that is
let loose
an ecstatic flutter of lungs
and stop.

Dead à Kempis—
they say he turned away from light.
Toward
is the truth.
Let us bury
our saints
and leave them to rot.
Let us love
the beautiful idea
of worms.

Then every juncture of tendon and bone
    the great bag of skin
        susceptible
to piercing spears
    connect
  to an axis
   spindle
  the infinite arms
     of a star
  and this spindle does what spindles do
    it spins
      and hurls
     radiant blue dust
   across the heavens
      a scintillating web
    that catches
 and eventually devours us
   in an end
    that is colorful
     and always exceeds
   the fallible eye.

Metaphysic, with Blue

There is a lake

Blue and deep and burial-cold.

Mountains that cup the lake;

The lake, a cup, a cup to hold, a cup that holds.

A cup to drink from,

Deep and cold.

Pines dwindle as they rise to scrabble and brush.

Blue to green to grey to sky to space to would you dare say God?

Dare say. All brutally empty until those bodies stripped in sunlight

And flung themselves beyond the rocky shore

Into a cold that bruised fingers and lips.

Blue and deep and cold,

Cold as burial, bruised and numb, cold as blue, as deep.

The bodies and rocks. Bodies, rocks,

Blue and cold.

Metaphysic, with Bird

A window allows
   that stories
     seldom
translate, that the verb falters.

O that it falters. And rises
   from mud again.
     That this window
allows a cardinal in the yard

to flash across a stretch of glass
   and vanish
     into eye and ear and heart
that follow feathers and light

to dreams of perfect bird,
   perfect cardinal
     in the yard
with mud and a verb—

to flash to fly to be
   to God. Verb falters
     when the window allows.
And rises.

Metaphysic, with Applebee's

Geese rise from the darkening lake.
Between the honk and feathery *whoosh,* they become the lake's memory
called ripple, lifted by something
that's also letting go
of the setting sun. Like this: I'm driving from the therapist,
from one of those agonies we try to wipe away with the tears,
throw away with wet mounds of Kleenex,
and shove away with purpose,
with something resembling hope, with hurry,
yes, always with hurry after those spendy hours of grief,
and today, there's traffic,
Memphis traffic,
a stoplight surrounded by the sprawl of suburbs and shops,
strip malls filled with The Gap, Eddie Bauer,
Blockbuster, and Applebee's.
You've been there.
The cars lock together, an exhaustive mess of go-nowhere,
and occasionally a honk, someone flipping the bird, or two cars
crumpling together in a fender bender,
and then without a flutter or thunder,
without music or lightning
or even a prophet's heralding cry,
all and each of the drivers, all and each of their passengers,
mothers and sons and uncles and friends and more,
the tense drivers clenching wheels
or banging drum solos with damp palms,
even the ones plunging fingers
deep into the retentive depths of their noses, all and each and more,
the screaming baby exciting itself to sweaty exhaustion,
the fat jogger in too-tight shorts, his walkman bumping out some
    motivational beat
echoed by the synchronized jiggle of jelloey thighs,

the drooling dogs hanging heads from back windows
or roasting on the flat beds
of trucks up from Mississippi,
all and each and more, the ice cream man, wary cyclist,
a grey squirrel skittering across a telephone line, and still more,
the manhole covers, a thrown-out Coke can
flattened in the street, bent bicycle rim, two red wrappers for French Fries,
each linty grain of filth and flesh and trash,
steel and plastic, wood, paper, dirt and dust
       strung together by silvery threads
which fuse into a tender palm of light.

No, I did not turn the car around
to ask for more information
on the benefits of medication. Someone honked,
and you know the rest: the signal turns from red to green, some people turn
    turn
to Applebee's to eat, and the stunning seraphim strings
turn into lines of traffic, the white hyphens
that lead away to measured lives,
and someone flipping the bird
or maybe car horns
recall, of course, the geese rising and flapping,
the geese gone, a lake, ripples, breeze dimpling
the water's skin,
and the transition back
to oh what a neat thing.
                     I say more.
If you see a man stopped in traffic, tears streaming
down his face, what will it take
to make you believe that he and you, all those I's
and its, the ugly and glorious things
we build and buy, think and feel, sell and hug and throw away
are light? Believe that even we,
creatures that cause such scarring pain,
beautiful jumbles of skin and bone, fumbled

intentions and the enduring silk of dreams,
are light?
                         Believe,
for all the Buicks and babies, Eddie Bauers and Applebee's,
for all the honked horns, plumes of exhaust, thoughts loosed through
    every head,
all the dejected excrement and holy hosts
of this blessed mess
shine. Yes, we shine.
Spears of grass piercing the sky, we shine; stars riven to clumpy mud, we
    shine;
birdsong sirening through the quivering leaves,
luminous blossoms sprouting
the lightning bolt of spring,
we shine,
o geese, o tears, o traffic, o yes,
we shine we love we light.

Emerson quotation from "An Address Delivered Before the Senior Class in Divinity College, Cambridge 1838."

In "Eclipse," the quotations from Hildegard of Bingen are either directly from her *Scivias* or variations based on her words. See *Hildegard of Bingen: Scivias,* translated by Mother Columba Hart and Jane Bishop (Paulist Press, New York, 1990). The quotations from Oswald Spengler in that poem come from his *Decline of the West* (Knopf, New York, 1939).

Oppen quotation from his poem "Of Being Numerous."

Robert Hass's "Against Botticelli" was important for the writing of "Botticelli."

Whitman quotation from his poem "Song of Myself."

In "After Kandinsky," the quotation is from Thomas à Kempis; the quotations throughout the rest of the poem are from Kandinsky's *Concerning the Spiritual in Art,* translated by M. T. H. Sadler (Dover Books, New York, 1977).

Lastly, the line "I say more" in "Metaphysic, with Applebee's" is borrowed, of course, from Gerard Manley Hopkins's "As kingfisher's catch fire."

ACKNOWLEDGMENTS

My thanks to the following journals in which these poems first appeared:

Bellowing Ark ("Breakfast")
Boulevard ("Choir")
Colorado Review ("Lightning,"; "Metaphysic, with Blue";
   Apollinaire on the Great Plains")
Denver Quarterly ("Botticelli"; "Of")
Interim ("Manifest and Destiny"; "St. Joan among the Pines";
   "Nocturne"; "Untitled")
The Iowa Review ("Eclipse"; "Yes, There Are Times")
Orphic Lute ("And This, Following the Weather")
Poetry East ("Prodigal")
Quarterly West ("After Kandinsky")
Volt ("Metaphysic, with Bird")

THE CONTEMPORARY POETRY SERIES

Edited by Paul Zimmer

Dannie Abse, *One-Legged on Ice*
Susan Astor, *Dame*
Gerald Barrax, *An Audience of One*
Tony Connor, *New and Selected Poems*
Franz Douskey, *Rowing Across the Dark*
Lynn Emanuel, *Hotel Fiesta*
John Engels, *Vivaldi in Early Fall*
John Engels, *Weather-Fear: New and Selected Poems, 1958–1982*
Brendan Galvin, *Atlantic Flyway*
Brendan Galvin, *Winter Oysters*
Michael Heffernan, *The Cry of Oliver Hardy*
Michael Heffernan, *To the Wreakers of Havoc*
Conrad Hilberry, *The Moon Seen as a Slice of Pineapple*
X. J. Kennedy, *Cross Ties*
Caroline Knox, *The House Party*
Gary Margolis, *The Day We Still Stand Here*
Michael Pettit, *American Light*
Bin Ramke, *White Monkeys*
J. W. Rivers, *Proud and on My Feet*
Laurie Sheck, *Amaranth*
Myra Sklarew, *The Science of Goodbyes*
Marcia Southwick, *The Night Won't Save Anyone*
Mary Swander, *Succession*
Bruce Weigl, *The Monkey Wars*
Paul Zarzyski, *The Make-Up of Ice*

THE CONTEMPORARY POETRY SERIES

Edited by Bin Ramke

Mary Jo Bang, *The Downstream Extremity of the Isle of Swans*
J. T. Barbarese, *New Science*
J. T. Barbarese, *Under the Blue Moon*
Cal Bedient, *The Violence of the Morning*
Stephanie Brown, *Allegory of the Supermarket*
Scott Cairns, *Figures for the Ghost*
Scott Cairns, *The Translation of Babel*
Richard Chess, *Tekiah*
Richard Cole, *The Glass Children*
Martha Collins, *A History of a Small Life on a Windy Planet*
Martin Corless-Smith, *Of Piscator*
Christopher Davis, *The Patriot*
Juan Delgado, *Green Web*
Wayne Dodd, *Echoes of the Unspoken*
Wayne Dodd, *Sometimes Music Rises*
Joseph Duemer, *Customs*
Candice Favilla, *Cups*
Casey Finch, *Harming Others*
Norman Finkelstein, *Restless Messengers*
Dennis Finnell, *Belovèd Beast*
Dennis Finnell, *The Gauguin Answer Sheet*
Karen Fish, *The Cedar Canoe*
Albert Goldbarth, *Heaven and Earth: A Cosmology*
Pamela Gross, *Birds of the Night Sky/Stars of the Field*
Kathleen Halme, *Every Substance Clothed*
Jonathan Holden, *American Gothic*
Paul Hoover, *Viridian*
Austin Hummell, *The Fugitive Kind*
Claudia Keelan, *The Secularist*
Joanna Klink, *They Are Sleeping*
Maurice Kilwein Guevara, *Postmortem*
Caroline Knox, *To Newfoundland*
Steve Kronen, *Empirical Evidence*
Patrick Lawler, *A Drowning Man Is Never Tall Enough*
Sydney Lea, *No Sign*

Jeanne Lebow, *The Outlaw James Copeland and the Champion-Belted Empress*

Phillis Levin, *Temples and Fields*

Gary Margolis, *Falling Awake*

Tod Marshall, *Dare Say*

Joshua McKinney, *Saunter*

Mark McMorris, *The Black Reeds*

Jacqueline Osherow, *Conversations with Survivors*

Jacqueline Osherow, *Looking for Angels in New York*

Tracy Philpot, *Incorrect Distances*

Paisley Rekdal, *A Crash of Rhinos*

Donald Revell, *The Gaza of Winter*

Martha Ronk, *Desire in L.A.*

Martha Ronk, *Eyetrouble*

Peter Sacks, *O Wheel*

Aleda Shirley, *Chinese Architecture*

Pamela Stewart, *The Red Window*

Susan Stewart, *The Hive*

Donna Stonecipher, *The Reservoir*

Terese Svoboda, *All Aberration*

Terese Svoboda, *Mere Mortals*

Lee Upton, *Approximate Darling*

Lee Upton, *Civilian Histories*

Arthur Vogelsang, *Twentieth Century Women*

Sidney Wade, *Empty Sleeves*

Liz Waldner, *Dark Would (The Missing Person)*

Marjorie Welish, *Casting Sequences*

Susan Wheeler, *Bag 'o' Diamonds*

C. D. Wright, *String Light*

Katayoon Zandvakili, *Deer Table Legs*

Andrew Zawacki, *By Reason of Breakings*

CPSIA information can be obtained
at www.ICGtesting.com
Printed in the USA
FSOW02n2106250916
25395FS